OCCASIONAL
P A P E R

Insurgency and Counterinsurgency in Iraq

Bruce Hoffman

OP-127-IPC/CMEPP

June 2004

RAND NATIONAL SECURITY RESEARCH DIVISION

This research in the public interest was funded by the U.S. government.

ISBN: 0-8330-3666-1

Published 2004 by the RAND Corporation
1700 Main Street, P.O. Box 2138, Santa Monica, CA 90407-2138
1200 South Hayes Street, Arlington, VA 22202-5050
201 North Craig Street, Suite 202, Pittsburgh, PA 15213-1516
RAND URL: http://www.rand.org/
To order RAND documents or to obtain additional information, contact
Distribution Services: Telephone: (310) 451-7002;
Fax: (310) 451-6915; Email: order@rand.org

Preface

The research presented here builds upon, and incorporates, past research undertaken at the RAND Corporation on insurgency and counterinsurgency, terrorism and counterterrorism, and related forms of nonconventional warfare—as well as on peacekeeping, nation-building, and stability operations. Among the previous RAND studies from which this paper particularly benefited are John Arquilla, David Ronfeldt, and Michele Zanini, "Networks, Netwar, and Information-Age Terrorism," in Ian O. Lesser et al., *Countering the New Terrorism* (MR-989-AF, 1999); James Dobbins et al., *America's Role in Nation-Building: From Germany to Iraq* (MR-1753-RC, 2003); Bruce Hoffman and Jennifer M. Taw, *A Strategic Framework for Countering Terrorism and Insurgency* (N-3506-DOS, 1992); Bruce Hoffman and Jennifer M. Taw, *Defense Policy and Low-Intensity Conflict: The Development of Britain's "Small Wars" Doctrine During the 1950s* (R-4501-A, 1991); Bruce Hoffman et al., *Lessons for Contemporary Counterinsurgencies: The Rhodesian Experience* (R-3998-USDP, 1991); James T. Quinlivan, "Burden of Victory: The Painful Arithmetic of Stability Operations," *RAND Review*, Vol. 27, No. 2 (Summer 2003); and Benjamin C. Schwarz, *American Counterinsurgency Doctrine and El Salvador: The Frustrations of Reform and the Illusions of Nation Building* (R-4042-USDP, 1991).

This research was funded by the U.S. government and conducted within the Intelligence Policy Center (IPC) and the Center for Middle East Public Policy (CMEPP) of the RAND National Security Research Division (NSRD). NSRD conducts research and analysis for the Office of the Secretary of Defense, the Joint Staff, the Unified Combatant Commands, the defense agencies, the Department of the Navy, the U.S. intelligence community, allied foreign governments, and foundations.

Comments are welcome and should be addressed to Dr. Bruce Hoffman at the RAND Corporation, 1200 South Hayes Street, Arlington, VA 22202-5050 or via email at hoffman@rand.org.

For more information on RAND's Intelligence Policy Center, contact the director, Kevin O'Connell. He can be reached by email at Kevin_O'Connell@rand.org; by phone at 310-393-0411, extension 5372; or by mail at RAND, 1700 Main Street, Santa Monica, California 90407-2138. More information about RAND is available at www.rand.org.

The RAND Corporation Quality Assurance Process

Peer review is an integral part of all RAND research projects. Prior to publication, this document, as with all documents in the RAND occasional paper series, was subject to a quality assurance process to ensure that the research meets several standards, including the following: The problem is well formulated; the research approach is well designed and well executed; the data and assumptions are sound; the findings are useful and advance knowledge; the implications and recommendations follow logically from the findings and are explained thoroughly; the documentation is accurate, understandable, cogent, and temperate in tone; the research demonstrates understanding of related previous studies; and the research is relevant, objective, independent, and balanced. Peer review is conducted by research professionals who were not members of the project team.

RAND routinely reviews and refines its quality assurance process and also conducts periodic external and internal reviews of the quality of its body of work. For additional details regarding the RAND quality assurance process, visit http://www.rand.org/ standards/.

Insurgency and Counterinsurgency in Iraq

"By the simple exercise of our will we can exert a power for good practically unbounded."
—Joseph Conrad, *Heart of Darkness*

In the 1993 film *Groundhog Day*, Bill Murray plays an arrogant television weatherman fated to relive the same day—February 2—and the same unedifying experiences over and over.[1] The eternal cycle of repetition in which Murray's character is condemned seems an apt parable to America's mostly ill-fated experiences in fighting insurgencies. More often than not, the United States has been frustrated in its efforts to effectively prosecute this unique blend of political-military operations. But, whereas Murray eventually rights his wayward path and attains true spiritual enlightenment, a similarly decisive epiphany has yet to occur with respect to America's historical ambivalence toward counterinsurgency. Indeed, an almost unbroken string of frustration (and disappointment) can be traced backward over nearly half a century from the situation in Iraq today to the early 1960s when the United States became heavily engaged in Indochina's wars. Vietnam and Iraq thus form two legs of a historically fraught triangle—with America's experiences in El Salvador in the 1980s providing the connecting leg.

The aim of this paper is not to rake over old coals or rehash now familiar criticism. Much has been written about past mistakes in Vietnam and El Salvador and more recently about the planning and implementation failures that have attended our current involvement in Iraq.[2] Rather, its purpose is to use the present as prologue in order to understand in coun-

This paper was researched and written during February 2004 and presented on 6 March 2004—that is, *before* the author had the opportunity to visit Iraq. He subsequently served as a senior adviser on counterterrorism and counterinsurgency to the Coalition Provisional Authority (CPA) in Baghdad from mid-March to mid-April. Although this paper contains neither new material nor reflections derived from the author's temporary duty assignment with CPA, the views and arguments expressed herein were both strengthened and validated by that experience.

This paper benefited tremendously from the incisive reviews provided by Lieutenant Colonel Fred T. Krawchuk, U.S. Army Special Forces, and RAND colleague Dr. Steven Hosmer. In addition, Professor Ian Beckett, Dr. Tom Marks, and Dr. Gordon McCormick—along with RAND colleagues both in Washington and Baghdad—provided many other helpful comments. It remains to be said that the opinions expressed and arguments presented are those of the author alone and that any errors or mistakes are entirely his responsibility as well.

[1] For an interesting account of how this film is used to illuminate spiritual real-life issues, see Alex Kuczynski, "Groundhog Almighty," *New York Times* (Sunday "Fashion and Style" section), 7 December 2003.

[2] See, for example, Anthony H. Cordesman, *Iraq: Too Uncertain to Call* (Washington, D.C.: Center for Strategic and International Studies, 14 November 2003; James Fallows, "Blind into Baghdad," *The Atlantic Monthly*, Vol. 293, No. 1 (January–February 2004), pp. 52–74; Joshua Hammer, "Tikrit Dispatch: Uncivil Military," *The New Republic*, 1 March 2004; Steven Metz, "Insurgency and Counterinsurgency in Iraq," *The Washington Quarterly*, Vol. 27, No. 1, Winter 2003–04; and David Rieff, "Blueprint for a Mess," *New York Times Magazine*, 2 November 2003.

terinsurgency terms where we have gone wrong in Iraq;[3] what unique challenges the current conflict in Iraq presents to the U.S. and other coalition military forces deployed there; and what light both shed on future counterinsurgency planning, operations, and requirements.[4]

The Ineluctable Political Dimension of Counterinsurgency

"You want me to write a fatwa for the Americans? I'll write one that tells them to get out of the country." —Fadil al-Kubaisy, Imam of the al Dawla al Kabeer mosque, Ramadi, Iraq[5]

At the foundation of counterinsurgency is the salience of the political dimension—in doctrine, planning, implementation, and, most importantly, operational coordination. Yet the failure to take this aspect of U.S. military operations in Iraq sufficiently into account arguably breathed life into the insurgency that emerged and has continued to gather momentum since last summer. At the heart of this criticism is the apparent neglect in the planning for post-invasion stability operations following the initial military assault on Iraq, the defeat of its military, and the destruction of Saddam Hussein and his dictatorial Ba'athist regime.[6] In a particularly piquant and trenchant analysis, Cordesman notes, "The fact remains . . . that the US government failed to draft a serious or effective plan for a 'Phase 4' of the war: The period of conflict termination and the creation of an effective national building office."[7] He goes on to quote a senior officer with intimate knowledge of the operation's planning and execution, who told Cordesman, "I can't judge the quality of the Phase 4 planning because I never really saw any."[8] Whether this was because no planning in fact was undertaken, as Cordesman argues (or, more likely, that planners either "were not given enough time to put together the best blueprint for what [was] called Phase IV—the ongoing reconstruction of Iraq"[9]), or because the importance of this phase of operations was not fully appreciated and therefore not initiated early enough,[10] is immaterial. The point is that this aspect of operations was woefully neglected.

Thus a critical window of opportunity was lost because of the failure to anticipate the widespread civil disorders and looting that followed the capture of Baghdad.[11] In something akin to a chain reaction, this failure was in turn further exacerbated by the operational dis-

---

[3] This is also the thrust of an article by Robert R. Tomes, "Relearning Counterinsurgency Warfare," *Parameters*, Spring 2004, pp. 16–17.

[4] Although the sources cited throughout this paper are published secondary scholarly sources or journalism accounts, the arguments presented here are based primarily on discussions held between December 2003 and February 2004 with serving American military and intelligence officers, U.S. and British officials in the CPA, and journalists who are currently in or have recently reported from Iraq.

[5] Quoted in Dexter Filkins, "Sunni Clerics Call for an End to Killing of Iraqis," *New York Times*, 1 March 2004.

[6] See Christopher Dickey, "Learning from the Pros," *Newsweek*, 16 January 2004; James Dobbins et al., *America's Role in Nation-Building: From Germany To Iraq* (Santa Monica, Calif.: The RAND Corporation, MR-1753-RC, 2003), pp. 167–222; Metz, "Insurgency and Counterinsurgency in Iraq," pp. 27–28; and Rieff, "Blueprint for a Mess."

[7] Cordesman, *Iraq: Too Uncertain to Call*, p. 2.

[8] Quoted in ibid.

[9] See Rowan Scarborough, "US Rushed Post-Saddam Planning," *Washington Times*, 3 September 2003.

[10] See the Letter to the Editor from Joseph J. Collins, Deputy Assistant Secretary of Defense, in response to Fallows, "Blind into Baghdad," published in the April 2004 issue of *The Atlantic Monthly* at http://www.theatlantic.com/issues/2004/04/letters.htm. The argument that plans were commissioned and prepared but not taken into account was substantiated in discussions with U.S. Department of Defense officials, April 2004.

[11] Fallows, "Blind into Baghdad," pp. 73–74; and Metz, "Insurgency and Counterinsurgency in Iraq," p. 27.

connects that have been cited between the Departments of Defense and State in pre-invasion/post-conflict planning and the inadequacy of the initial ORHA (Organization for Reconstruction and Humanitarian Assistance) effort[12] that, many argue, today continue to plague civilians in the Coalition Provisional Authority (CPA) and U.S. military commanders.[13] These initial missteps seriously undermined the U.S. effort in Iraq and arguably led to the uncertain situation in that country today. That they are now recognized (albeit, only slowly) and are being corrected has doubtless prevented Iraq from sliding further into violence and instability—but the damage already was done.[14] This is why Cordesman titled his analysis, released last November, *Iraq: Too Uncertain to Call.* "The bad news," he wrote,

> is that the US sowed many of the seeds of both the present low intensity war and many of the current uncertainties in Iraq. The good news is that the US has since made major efforts to restructure its military forces to fight the emerging threat, has set up a more effective effort to create a new government, and has funded and begun to implement a major aid program. One reason it is so difficult to judge whether the cup is half empty or half full, is that the US has only begun to pour.[15]

While it can be argued that U.S. military planners could not have been expected to anticipate the emergence of an insurgency any more than they could have foreseen the widespread disorders, looting, and random violence that followed the fall of Baghdad, that is precisely the nub of the problem.[16] The fact that military planners apparently didn't consider the possibility that sustained and organized resistance could gather momentum and transform itself into an insurgency reflects a pathology that has long afflicted governments and militaries everywhere: the failure not only to recognize the incipient conditions for insurgency, but also to ignore its nascent manifestations and arrest its growth before it is able to gain initial traction and in turn momentum. Indeed, this was among the central conclusions of a 1991 RAND study that examined Britain's variegated experiences in countering insurgencies during the 1950s. "Late recognition of an insurgency," the report stated, "is costly, insofar as the insurgents have the opportunity to gain a foothold before facing any organized opposition."[17] A follow-on RAND effort, which this time analyzed seven case studies involving counterinsurgency and counterterrorist efforts (including a reexamination of the aforementioned three British campaigns of the 1950s) reached an identical conclusion.[18] The failure to detect early on the signs of incipient insurgency, combined with initially hesitant

---

[12] Rieff, "Blueprint for a Mess."

[13] Email communications with a senior CPA official, Baghdad, Iraq, January and February 2004. See also Joshua Hammer, "Tikrit Dispatch: Uncivil Military," *The New Republic,* 1 March 2004.

[14] As one U.S. Army officer involved in countering the insurgency observes, the real problem is that success "demands co-ordinated military, political, informational and economic efforts to remove the fundamental sources of strength—it is here where we are encountering our greatest difficulties." Quoted in Vernon Loeb, "Rumsfeld Seeks Better Intelligence on Iraqi Insurgents," *Washington Post,* 11 December 2003.

[15] Cordesman, *Iraq: Too Uncertain to Call,* p. 3.

[16] See Brian Knowlton, "Iraq Resistance Lasting Longer Than Expected, Powell Concedes," *International Herald Tribune* (Paris), 26 October 2003; and Lizette Alvarez, "British Official Sees No Early Exit from Iraq," *New York Times,* 5 January 2004.

[17] Bruce Hoffman and Jennifer M. Taw, *Defense Policy and Low-Intensity Conflict: The Development of Britain's "Small Wars" Doctrine During the 1950s* (Santa Monica, Calif.: The RAND Corporation, R-4501-A, 1991), p. vii.

[18] The three key British counterterrorist/counterinsurgency campaigns of the 1940s and 1950s involving Malaya, Kenya, and Cyprus; the more recent struggle in Northern Ireland (though covering only the period between 1969 and 1991); the 1965–1980 Rhodesian conflict; and the counterterrorist experiences of Germany and Italy during the 1970s and 1980s. See Bruce Hoffman and Jennifer M. Taw, *A Strategic Framework for Countering Terrorism and Insurgency* (Santa Monica, Calif.: The RAND Corporation, N-3506-DOS, 1992).

and uncoordinated responses in terms of meshing political as well as military approaches, gave the insurgents or terrorists invaluable time to entrench themselves in the civilian population and solidify their efforts while the security forces groped and stumbled about. By the time the authorities realized the seriousness of the emergent situation, it was already too late.[19] This is not to say that progress and success remained entirely elusive for Britain, but that invaluable opportunities were squandered to bring the insurgency immediately to heel and time, money, and, most of all, lives were needlessly expended.[20]

As Cordesman and other observers widely agree, considerable progress in the political or "hearts and minds" dimension of counterinsurgency has been made in Iraq in recent months. Such efforts have included improving access to vital services (electricity, water, etc.), reopening schools, establishing an Iraqi police force, restoring the country's oil production, and generally encouraging normal daily commerce. However, the general unevenness and inconsistency of these achievements, and the fact that for many Iraqis many of these improvements are either too little or too late or both, has created cynicism, animosity, enmity, and worse.[21] All or at least some of this might otherwise have been avoided by better planning and foresight. Indeed, by October, polls in Iraq were showing a marked decline in the number of persons who viewed the U.S. and other coalition forces as liberators and indeed that the majority of Iraqis now regarded them as occupiers.[22]

A supposedly well-known military aphorism asserts, "Ignoring the civil side of counterinsurgency . . . [is like] playing chess while the enemy is playing poker." As Major John Nagl, the operations officer in the 1st Infantry Division and an expert on counterinsurgency (having taught at West Point and published an insightful book on the subject),[23] told a reporter last December, this critical civil side of insurgency "is not being applied in Iraq as well as it could be."[24] However typical or atypical, an account published in the *New York Times* last November about the shooting deaths in Mosul of two American soldiers chillingly underscored the fragility of Iraqi–American relations. "[W]hen word came Sunday afternoon that two American soldiers had been shot in the head and killed a block away," Dexter Filkins reported,

> the men of Ras al Jada fire station ran to the site and looked on with glee as a crowd of locals dragged the Americans from their car and tore off their watches and jackets and boots.
>
> 'I was happy, everyone was happy,' Waadallah Muhammad, one of the firefighters, said as he stood in front of the firehouse. 'The Americans, yes, they do good things, but only to enhance their reputation. They are occupiers. We want them to leave.'[25]

---

[19] Ibid., p. 6.

[20] Ibid., pp. vi, 3–6, and 77–78.

[21] See, for example, Alex Berenson, "A Baghdad Neighborhood, Once Hopeful, Now Reels as Iraq's Turmoil Persists," *New York Times*, 14 December 2003; Roger Cohen, "Iraq and Its Patron, Growing Apart," *New York Times*, 21 December 2003; Knights and White, "Iraqi resistance proves resilient," p. 24; Metz, "Insurgency and Counterinsurgency in Iraq," pp. 27–28; and Rieff, "Blueprint for a Mess."

[22] H.D.S. Greenway, "U.S. Policy in Iraq Stirs Muslim Animosity," *Boston Globe*, 31 October 2003.

[23] John A. Nagl, *Counterinsurgency Lessons from Malaya to Vietnam: Learning to Eat Soup with a Knife* (Westport, Conn., and London: Praeger, 2002).

[24] Peter Maass, "Professor Nagl's War," *New York Times Sunday Magazine*, 11 January 2004.

[25] Dexter Filkins, "Attacks on G.I.'s in Mosul Rise as Good Will Fades," *New York Times*, 27 November 2003.

As Lieutenant General Ricardo Sanchez, the American military commander in Iraq, conceded exactly a week earlier, "much work remained to be done in winning 'hearts and minds'" in Iraq.[26] Similarly, the claim of Ambassador L. Paul Bremer, the top U.S. civilian administrator in Iraq, nearly a month after the above incident occurred, that the CPA is "going to be very aggressive with our information campaign" is an example of the right intentions and right policy but also of time and opportunities undeniably—and needlessly—lost.[27]

The critical nexus between the political and military dimensions has been widely acknowledged even by those practitioners of counterinsurgency whose means and methods once aroused the ire not only of human rights activists in various nongovernmental oversight organizations but of the U.S. government as well. For example, General Rene Emilio Ponce, the defense minister at the height of the insurgency in El Salvador during the 1980s, was often quoted as stating that "90 percent" of countering insurgency "is political, social, economic and ideological and only 10 percent military."[28] Given the massive extent of American support of the Salvadoran counterinsurgency effort,[29] it is not surprising perhaps that one of its main benefactors should wax eloquently about this critical political-military dynamic. Nonetheless, from almost the beginning of when U.S. counterinsurgency doctrine and implementation was being framed in the early 1960s, this ineluctable link was clearly recognized. President Kennedy stressed precisely this same point at the very outset of the significant escalation of U.S. assistance to the Government of South Vietnam that commenced during his administration. According to Roger Hilsman, who was responsible for counterinsurgency policy at the State Department during the Kennedy administration and himself had direct experience of such warfare as an officer in the Office of Strategic Services (OSS) during World War II, from the time that JFK took office in January 1961, the new president was preoccupied not just with counterinsurgency but with its critical political element. "What are we doing about guerrilla warfare?" Hilsman quotes JFK asking him shortly after he took up residence in the White House. The president then answered his own question, stating that "new military tactics had to be developed . . . But new political tactics also had to be devised, and, most importantly, the two—the military and political—had to be meshed together and blended."[30]

Kennedy's view closely reflected British military thinking on the subject. Surprisingly, though, Britain itself had only recently—and not very readily—come to the same conclusion. During the 15 years that followed World War II, Britain had become enmeshed in a succession of counterinsurgency campaigns involving different environments (urban and ru-

---

[26] John F. Burns, "Witness: The New Iraq Is Grim, Hopeful and Still Scary," *New York Times*, 16 November 2003.

[27] Quoted in Cohen, "Iraq and Its Patron, Growing Apart."

[28] Quoted in Benjamin C. Schwarz, *American Counterinsurgency Doctrine and El Salvador: The Frustrations of Reform and the Illusions of Nation Building* (Santa Monica, Calif.: The RAND Corporation, R-4042-USDP, 1991), p. 22. Schwarz writes that Ponce previously "served as chief of personnel and later as deputy director (essentially commander under an inactive director) of the Treasury Police—the unit of the Salvadoran armed forces most notorious for its sadistic and particularly extravagant crushing of dissent—from 1979 to 1982, the height of the period of political violence in El Salvador . . . and was in fact denied a U.S. visa for years because of suspicion of human rights abuse." Footnote 12, p. 22.

[29] Between 1980 and 1990 the United States poured more than $4.5 billion into El Salvador ($1.3 billion in the form of direct military assistance and over $850 million in unsubsidized credits—excluding an estimated CIA investment of over $500 million) in an effort to defeat the communist insurgency there. American training teams and advisory personnel also oversaw the fivefold expansion, equipping, and training of the 57,000-man Salvadoran armed forces during this time period. See ibid., pp. xiii and 2; and, Bruce Hoffman et al., *Lessons for Contemporary Counterinsurgencies: The Rhodesian Experience* (Santa Monica, Calif.: The RAND Corporation, R-3998-USDP, 1991), p. 2.

[30] Nagl, *Counterinsurgency Lessons from Malaya to Vietnam*, p. 124.

ral as well as jungle and mountain) against a variety of opponents (anticolonialists, communist revolutionaries, and ethno-nationalist separatists) in places as diverse as Palestine, Malaya, Kenya, and Cyprus. Counterinsurgency, née imperial policing, tactics developed to suppress earlier colonial insurrections throughout the 18th, 19th, and early 20th centuries were often readily adaptable to subsequent mid-20th century campaigns.[31] Nevertheless, when the British found themselves embroiled in overseas internal security commitments after World War II, they were completely unprepared. Training exercises for troops sent to Malaya and Kenya, for example, continued to be based on lessons drawn from the conventional campaigns of World War II. The little time devoted to counterinsurgency training mostly consisted of executing outmoded, heavy-handed "cordon and search" operations. This tactic had in fact already been discredited by Britain's experience in Palestine during the late 1940s because of the widespread disruption to daily life and commerce among the civilian population and the anger and resentment toward the authorities that such operations engendered, though this passed unnoticed in subsequent British campaigns.[32] That U.S. military forces in Iraq have similarly applied this tactic with similar results—alienating the Iraqi civilian population[33]—underscores the overwhelming organizational tendency *not* to absorb historical lessons from previous counterinsurgencies when planning and conducting this particular mode of warfare.

It is interesting to note that this pathologic resistance on the part of the military to "lessons learned" on counterinsurgency (and counterterrorism for that matter) rarely afflicts the opponents in a given conflict (i.e., guerrilla groups or terrorist organizations), who consciously study and learn both from their own past mistakes as well as from the successful operations of their enemies. This is no less true among insurgents in Iraq than it has been for guerrillas and terrorists elsewhere.[34] Indeed, this same point was made last July by General John Abizaid, the commanding general of the U.S. Central Command, responsible for all military operations in Iraq. The insurgency, he asserted, "is getting more organized, and it is learning. It is adapting, it is adapting to our tactics, techniques and procedures, and we've got to adapt to their tactics, techniques and procedures."[35]

In Britain's case, it was not until the late 1950s—a decade after Palestine had ended and Malaya had started, and while Britain was already heavily involved in both Kenya and Cyprus—that its military strategists, planners, and doctrine-writers realized the extent to which they had gutted their colonial-era counterinsurgency capabilities. Although the British eventually were able to formulate a series of responses adaptable to various contingencies, they nevertheless repeated the same errors in judgment and organization at the onset of each new insurgency.[36] For the British, many of the initial problems and lack of success they expe-

---

[31] John Pimlott, "The British Army," in Ian Beckett and John Pimlott (eds.), *Armed Forces and Modern Counter-Insurgency* (New York: St. Martin's Press, 1985), pp. 16–17.

[32] Hoffman and Taw, *Defense Policy and Low-Intensity Conflict*, p. 1.

[33] Dexter Filkins, "Dual Role of GI's difficult to juggle," *International Herald Tribune* (Paris), 3 November 2003; and Michael Knights and Jeffrey White, "Iraqi resistance proves resilient," *Jane's Intelligence Review*, November 2003, p. 24; and P. Mitchell Prothero, "Iraqi Guerrillas: 'Why we fight'," *United Press International*, 4 December 2003.

[34] See, for example, John S. White, U.S. Army NGIC, *NGIC Assessment: Adoption of Asymmetrical TTPs by Anti-Coalition Fighters in Iraq*, 30 July 2003; Brian Bennett and Michael Ware, "Life Behind Enemy Lines: An inside look at the Ba'athists, terrorists, Islamists and disaffected Iraqis fighting U.S. Troops," *Time* (New York), 15 December 2003, p. 27; and Bruce Hoffman, *Inside Terrorism* (New York: Columbia University Press, 1998), pp. 180–183.

[35] Quoted in Brian Knowlton, "Top U.S. General in Iraq Sees 'Classical Guerrilla-Type' War," *International Herald Tribune* (Paris), 16 July 2003.

[36] Hoffman and Taw, *Defense Policy and Low-Intensity Conflict*, p. 2.

rienced successively in Malaya, Kenya, and Cyprus were overcome by the recognition of how critical political-military coordination was in waging an effective counterinsurgency. The approach that they eventually adapted is not without relevance to America's current involvement in Iraq: involving the implementation of a single, unified policy and command authority that knitted together the political and military dimensions. Authority over the course of each counterinsurgency was delegated to a single British representative who was either a retired or serving British flag officer (e.g., General Sir Gerald Templer in Malaya and Field Marshal Sir John Harding in Cyprus) but who nonetheless was thoroughly cognizant of, and committed to, waging the political as well as military efforts against the insurgents.[37] This measure effectively solved the problems of bureaucratic rivalries, disconnects, and infighting thereby permitting the effective coordination of the civil administration, the military, and the police; the coordination of intelligence; and, most critically, the flexibility to respond quickly, often with novel policies and tactics, to the problems at hand.[38]

Nearly half a century later, these principles are enshrined in British Army counterinsurgency doctrine. For example, the introduction to the counterinsurgency section of *Army Field Manual, vol. V, Operations Other Than War* (1995) begins with a quote from General Sir Frank Kitson, one of the best known exponents of the "British School" of counterinsurgency. Kitson emphatically states, "The first thing that must be apparent when contemplating the sort of action which a government facing insurgency should take, is that there can be no such thing as a purely military solution because insurgency is not primarily a military activity."[39] The doctrine's statement of the fundamental principles of counterinsurgency is itself pointedly titled "A Matter of Balance." It states unequivocally:

> There has never been a purely military solution to revolution; political, social, economic and military measures all have a part to play in restoring the authority of a legitimate government. The security forces act in support of the civil authority in a milieu in which there is less certainty than in conventional war. The problem is that, working on insufficient information, at least in the early stages, decisions have to be made affecting every aspect of political, economic and social life in the country. These decisions have repercussions for the nation far beyond its borders, both in the diplomatic field and in the all-important sphere of public opinion.

Indeed, first among the six counterinsurgency principles defined by British doctrine is the "Political Primacy and Political Aim" followed by:

- Coordinated Government Machinery
- Intelligence and Information
- Separating the Insurgent from This Support
- Neutralising the Insurgent
- Longer Term Post-Insurgency Planning.[40]

Given that the U.S. global war on terrorism may likely require future nation-building efforts in similarly violent, polarized, and tyrannically ruled countries like Iraq, the ability of

---

[37] Hoffman and Taw, *A Strategic Framework for Countering Terrorism and Insurgency*, pp. 9–10, 13–15.

[38] Hoffman and Taw, *Defense Policy and Low-Intensity Conflict*, p. vi.

[39] Quoted in DGD&D 18/34/56 Army Code No 71596 (Pts 1 & 2), *Army Field Manual, vol. V, Operations Other Than War*, "Section B: Counter Insurgency Operations, Part 2 The Conduct of Counter Insurgency Operations," (London: Prepared under the direction of the Chief of the General Staff, 1995), p. 3-1.

[40] Ibid., pp. 3-1 to 3-2.

the American military similarly to overcome or obviate such institutional pathologies regarding counterinsurgency as the British once did is not without relevance.[41] Indeed, in the case of the U.S. Marine Corps, lessons from the British experience had already figured prominently in their planning for postwar stability operations in Iraq. The Marines were reported to have "consult[ed] with British officers about their experiences in Belfast over the decades" before deployment. "We've changed our tactics midstream," said one Marine liaison officer assigned to the populated areas in and around Nasiriyah, Iraq.[42] The Marine example in fact testifies to the general ossification of counterinsurgency doctrine, training, and planning that has long been overshadowed by other priorities and requirements in U.S. military strategy and tactics. Indeed, perhaps the seminal American encapsulation of the essentials of counterinsurgency is the Marines' *Small Wars Manual*,[43] which was first published in 1940, reprinted in 1987, and has been republished and studied since. This honorable exception to the seemingly continuous process of rediscovery and reinvention of the counterinsurgency wheel[44] interestingly devotes an entire chapter to "Relationship with the State Department"—with the first section specifically addressing the "Importance of cooperation."[45]

The U.S. military is, however, learning from past operational missteps and setbacks in Afghanistan. In December 2003, for instance, Lieutenant General David Barno, the commander of the American-led coalition force in Afghanistan, announced a new strategy involving, among other things, the expansion of military provincial reconstruction teams throughout the country. These teams would provide reconstruction and humanitarian assistance as part of a concerted "hearts and minds" effort[46] in tandem with other units who would play an active role in the renewed hunt for bin Laden by being stationed in Afghan villages for periods of time. The reasoning behind this move is that "by becoming a more permanent, familiar presence . . . they hope to be able to receive and act on intelligence within hours."[47] In Iraq as well, Marine units being deployed there in early 2004 had similarly been planning to position themselves among the population in their areas of operation—including in the notoriously violent Sunni Triangle. In tactics reminiscent of the Combined Action Platoons of the Vietnam War, a Marine officer responsible for planning explained that the "idea is that this Platoon, similar to Vietnam, will live and work with the Police and ICDC [Iraqi Civil Defense Corps]."[48] According to one report of the lessons that the Marines have drawn from the situation in Iraq during the period the insurgency gathered momentum between August and December 2003, "Marine officers said they are also aiming for more restraint in the use of force and intend to limit the use of heavy weapons, using

---

[41] As Nagl notes, this is an institutional pattern of behavior in the U.S. Army transcending half a century. See *Counterinsurgency Lessons from Malaya to Vietnam*, p. 6.

[42] Quoted in Peter Baker, "Tactics Turn Unconventional; Commanders Draw Lessons of Belfast in Countering Attacks," *Washington Post*, 30 March 2003. See also Maass, "Professor Nagl's War."

[43] U.S. Marine Corps, *Small Wars Manual* (reprint of 1940 edition) (Washington, D.C.: U.S. Government Printing Office, 1940), passim.

[44] Bruce Hoffman, "Current Research on Terrorism and LIC," *Studies in Conflict and Terrorism*, Vol. 15, No. 1 (1992), p. 31.

[45] U.S. Marine Corps, *Small Wars Manual*, pp. 33–34.

[46] Carlotta Gall, "U.S. Military Unveils Changes in Strategy in Afghanistan," *New York Times*, 21 December 2003.

[47] David E. Sanger and Eric Schmitt, "New U.S. Effort Steps up Hunt for bin Laden," *New York Times*, 29 February 2004.

[48] Quoted in Thomas E. Ricks, "Marines to Offer New Tactics in Iraq: Reduced Use of Force Planned After Takeover from Army," *Washington Post*, 7 January 2004.

bombs and weapons as a last resort. That contrasts with Army operations, in which air strikes and artillery were sometimes used to intimidate at the outset of confrontations."[49]

In fairness to the U.S. Army, it should be emphasized that lessons were also learned and operations adjusted to address more specifically the political dimension of counterinsurgency. For example, in the north of Iraq, Major General David H. Petraeus, the commander of the 101st Airborne Division based in Mosul, undertook precisely the types of innovative approaches with respect to the Iraqi civilian population and newly constituted Iraqi security forces long advocated by British doctrine and at the heart of effective counterinsurgency operations.[50] His main constraints were insufficient funds to accomplish all he had hoped and intended[51] and some friction with the CPA.[52] The problem, accordingly, seemed less not knowing what to do, than a flawed and mostly uneven application of counterinsurgency doctrine. As one senior CPA official explains,

> Some of these commanders have paid close attention to the lessons learned over the years [about countering insurgency] and are applying them in theater but it is not division or battalion wide. It often is up to the individual commanders. For instance the 2BCT Baghdad of the 1AD here is doing it 3 different ways dependant upon the commander of the individual unit. One is using lots of low level intel ideas coupled with a get on the ground approach that is paying high dividends. The other two don't care and just go about business as usual.[53]

So can conventional militaries effectively execute counterinsurgency missions without the extensive training that is *de rigueur* for special operations forces (SOF)? Judging from the U.S. military's experiences in Iraq, the answer is at best far from clear and at worst that they cannot. The problem in fact may be more one involving systemic changes in doctrine, organizational mind-set, and institutional ethos than mere additional training opportunities—no matter how detailed or extensive. As one U.S. Army Special Forces officer laments: "CT [counterterrorism] and COIN are the bread and butter of SOF, but SOF is a minority voice within a largely conventional military."[54]

The Fundamental Military and Intelligence Dimensions of Counterinsurgency

> *"You're the reason for the explosions! You're the reason! God's curses on you!"*
> —Security guard at the Shi'a mosque in Karbala, Iraq, where suicide bombers struck during the annual festival of Ashura on March 2, 2004 [55]

While emphasizing the political side of counterinsurgency, Kitson was equally mindful of the fundamental military side of this equation. Indeed, Kitson forcefully stresses that "there is no

---

[49] Ibid. This point is corroborated by a senior CPA official, Baghdad, Iraq. Email communication, January 2004.

[50] See Hammer, "Tikrit Dispatch: Uncivil Military."

[51] Discussion with serving U.S. Army officer directly familiar with General Petraeus's initiatives, U.S. Military Academy, West Point, New York, February 2004.

[52] Hammer, "Tikrit Dispatch: Uncivil Military."

[53] Email communication with senior CPA official, Baghdad, Iraq, January 2004.

[54] U.S. Army Special Forces officer, email communication with the author, May 2004.

[55] The accusation was directed at foreign journalists with the guard blaming the United States, according to the journalists, for its "inability to bring order" to Iraq, quoted in Anthony Shadid, "For Pilgrims, Horror on a Holy Day," *Washington Post*, 3 March 2004.

such thing as a wholly political solution either, short of surrender, because the very fact that a state of insurgency exists implies that violence is involved which will have to be countered to some extent at least by the use of force."[56] Essential to the effective application of that force is the acquisition of actionable intelligence, its rapid and proper analysis, and, perhaps most critically, its efficacious coordination and dissemination.[57] Kitson himself, in his magisterial work *Low Intensity Operations*, emphasizes the importance of the intelligence process. "If it is accepted that the problem of defeating the enemy consists very largely of finding him, it is easy to recognize the paramount importance of good information."[58]

One of the elemental imperatives of intelligence in counterinsurgency, according to Julian Paget—who served as a lieutenant-colonel in the British Army and, together with Kitson, is considered one of Britain's foremost experts on the subject—is that "every effort must be made to know the Enemy before the insurgency begins."[59] But intelligence was wanting because every such effort was in fact *not* made, resulting in the failure to anticipate the violence and resistance that gradually escalated throughout last spring and summer. Even though, according to the *Washington Post*, the CIA station in Iraq now has more than 300 full-time case officers and nearly 500 persons in total (including contractors) compared with its originally planned complement of just 85 officers, problems in intelligence collection reportedly remain. According to the *Post*, the CIA mission there is thus the "largest . . . in the world, and the biggest since Saigon during Vietnam 30 years ago." Nonetheless, despite both this significant expansion and redirection of effort to the insurgency, senior intelligence officials and others claim that "it has had little success penetrating the resistance and identifying foreign terrorists involved in the insurgency."[60]

The inadequacies in intelligence on the insurgents can also be attributed to the focus on the search for Iraqi stockpiles of weapons of mass destruction (WMD). Indeed, it was not until late November—when the daily pace of guerrilla attacks on American troops rose to some 40 per day—that intelligence officers and analysts were reassigned to focus on the insurgency.[61] The inexperience of American forces in counterinsurgency operations and the failure of pre-invasion plans and post-invasion policy to take into account the possibility of violence and resistance firstly occurring, much less escalating into insurgency, is likely another reason. Cordesman, for example, reports that when in November he visited the 1st Armored Division, responsible for Baghdad and the Green Zone,

> The unit was not trained or equipped for the mission when it arrived. . . . The division has had to change its whole operating style after 20 years of focusing on fighting conventional heavy forces. It has had to develop HUMINT procedures and turn away from reliance on technical intelligence sources. Even now it needs twice as many HUMINT teams as it has . . .

> The unit feels that intelligence is the key to success. It was slow to fully organize and create suitable data bases, learn how to run sources, find out what sources were reli-

---

[56] DGD&D, *Army Field Manual, vol. V, Operations Other Than War*, p. 3-1.

[57] Hoffman and Taw, *A Strategic Framework for Countering Terrorism and Insurgency*, p. 77.

[58] Frank Kitson, *Low Intensity Operations: Subversion, Insurgency, Peacekeeping* (London: Faber and Faber, 1971), p. 95.

[59] Julian Paget, *Counter-Insurgency Campaigning* (London: Faber and Faber, 1967), pp. 163–164.

[60] Dana Priest, "Violence, Turnover Blunt CIA Effort in Iraq," *Washington Post*, 4 March 2004.

[61] This entailed the reassignment of the linguists, analysts, and other experts serving in the 1,400-person Iraq Survey Group to the counterinsurgency mission from the search for WMD. See Douglas Jehl, "U.S. to Shift Some Experts from Arms to Anti-terror," *New York Times*, 27 November 2003.

able and what sources work. A lack of translators and trained intelligence personnel was and is a problem.[62]

Indeed, no less an authority than General Abizaid has proclaimed that the U.S. forces require "better and more timely intelligence to crush those responsible for the roadside bombings, ambushes and mortar attacks."[63]

But perhaps the most important reason that the intelligence was inadequate concerns the "lesser-included contingency" status with which counterinsurgency in the U.S. military has long been accorded. Here, again, it is appropriate to cite Kitson's views on the subject when he writes in *Low Intensity Operations* about the necessity of "attuning men's minds to cope with the environment of this sort of war."[64] Interestingly, the identical point is made by Joaquin Villalobos, the Salvadoran former guerrilla leader who now teaches at Oxford University and also advises Colombian president Alvaro Uribe about his country's counterinsurgency strategy. For Villalobos, the solution to America's historical problems with counterinsurgency in general and with the intelligence needed to counter insurgencies in particular is clear. "The United States needs to transform its soldiers, its officers, its doctrines to adapt to this kind of war," he believes.

According to Christopher Dickey, the veteran *Newsweek* correspondent who covered the Nicaraguan[65] and Salvadoran insurgencies, as well as the Palestinian intifadas and terrorism and guerrilla warfare around the globe, and is a keen and insightful observer of these types of conflicts short of war,

> What we need in fact are figures more or less like Colonel Creighton, the ethnographer-scholar-soldier in *Kim*, Rudyard Kipling's great novel about spies and insurgents in colonial India. As the late Edward Said once wrote, 'Creighton sees the world from a totally systematic viewpoint. Everything about India interests him, because everything in it is significant for his rule.

> Instead, we have tens of thousands of men and women getting on-the-job training under fire. It's a credit to our soldiers that they've managed to learn as much as they have about the people on the patches of turf they've occupied these last 10 months. And you can see the payoff with increased intelligence leading to the capture of, among others, Saddam. But this spring, just about all of those weary, experienced soldiers are due to be rotated home . . . and those who replace them will, in most cases, have to start all over again figuring out where they are, what they are doing there and who those folks are staring at them across the concertina wire.[66]

In no area is the intelligence lacuna more acute in Iraq than in the determination of insurgent identity and numbers—two of the most basic criteria. "We are quite blind there," the head of a European intelligence service monitoring developments in Iraq complained last November. "The Americans and Brits know very little about this enemy."[67] This poverty of

---

[62] Anthony H. Cordesman, *The Current Military Situation in Iraq* (Washington, D.C.: Center for Strategic and International Studies, 14 November 2003), pp. 13–14.

[63] Eric Schmitt and David E. Sanger, "Guerrillas Posing More Danger, Says U.S.," *New York Times*, 13 November 2003.

[64] Kitson, *Low Intensity Operations*, p. 165.

[65] Author of, among other works, *With the Contras: A Reporter in the Wilds of Nicaragua* (New York: Simon & Schuster, 1987).

[66] Dickey, "Learning from the Pros."

[67] Don Van Natta, Jr. and Desmond Butler, "Hundreds of militants head to Iraq for Jihad," *International Herald Tribune* (Paris), 3 November 2003.

definitive, much less clear, knowledge about our opponents in Iraq underscores Paget's admonition to "know the Enemy." A figure of 5,000 Iraqi insurgents or FREs (for Former Regime Elements, also referred to as FRLs, for Former Regime Loyalists)—mostly Sunni Muslims who belonged to the Ba'ath Party or served in the military, police, or security and intelligence services—was cited by General Abizaid in November and appears to be the generally accepted number.[68] It is also widely claimed that "95% of the attacks"[69] or "95% of the threat"[70] or "over 90% of the violent insurgents"[71] consist(s) of FREs—who either carry out attacks themselves or pay others to do so. It is increasingly reported that hired criminals or unemployed "angry young men" are being paid by FREs to attack U.S. forces.[72] And, according to Major General Raymond T. Odierno, the commander of the Army's 4th Infantry Division, the bounty on attacks on coalition military targets is rising. "When we first got here," he explained in an October interview with the press, "we believed it was about $100 to conduct an attack against coalition forces, and $500 if you're successful. We now believe it's somewhere between $1,000 and $2,000 if you conduct an attack, and $3,000 to $5,000 if you're successful."[73]

These assertions mostly dovetail with what Cordesman was told when he visited the 4th Infantry a month later. Indeed, he was informed that some 70–80 percent of captured insurgents in that unit's area of operations were paid attackers—among them criminals freed by Hussein during the invasion. Cordesman's information diverges from these claims, however, in the area of local FREs versus foreign jihadists. For example, in the Division's operational area, he was told, "[a]lmost all the threat is local FREs. All claim, however, that the threat is foreign"[74]—thus raising the crucial question of the number of non-Iraqis summoned to that country for the purpose of jihad. The paucity of accurate information on precisely this subject was cited by Ambassador Bremer as well. "The most critical problem," Bremer reportedly stated, according to Cordesman's notes of the briefing, "is intelligence. Still weak on both FRLs and foreigners. . . . Are getting better but still major problems in HUMINT collection and analysis . . . Do not have a reliable picture of who is organizing attacks, or the size and structure of various elements."[75]

In this respect, estimates of the number of foreign fighters in Iraq range widely from the low hundreds to the low thousands.[76] According to U.S. and coalition military sources on the one hand, approximately 200–400 foreign fighters are thought to be fighting in

---

[68] Marianne Brun-Rovet, "Insurgents are 'few in number but organised'," *Financial Times* (London), 14 November 2003. See also, Schmitt and Sanger, "Guerrillas Posing More Danger, Says U.S."; and Jehl, "U.S. to Shift Some Experts from Arms to Anti-terror."

[69] Ambassador Bremer cited in Cordesman, *The Current Military Situation in Iraq*, p. 2.

[70] Major General Raymond T. Odierno cited in Raymond Bonner and Joel Brinkley, "Latest Attacks Underscore Differing Intelligence Estimates of Strength of Foreign Guerrillas," *New York Times*, 28 October 2003.

[71] John E. McLaughlin, Deputy Director of Central Intelligence quoted in Dana Priest, "The CIA's 'Anonymous' No. 2: Low-Profile Director Leads Agency's Analytical Side," *Washington Post*, 9 January 2004.

[72] General Abizaid quoted in Schmitt and Sanger, "Guerrillas Posing More Danger, Says U.S." See also Brun-Rovet, "Insurgents are 'few in number but organised.'"

[73] Quoted in Bonner and Brinkley, "Latest Attacks Underscore Differing Intelligence Estimates of Strength of Foreign Guerrillas." See also Maass, "Professor Nagl's War."

[74] Cordesman, *The Current Military Situation in Iraq*, p. 25.

[75] Ibid., p. 2.

[76] See reports such as those from June that cited American military commanders' assertions that "foreign fighters are being actively recruited by loyalists to Saddam Hussein to join the resistance against American forces in Iraq." Michael R. Gordon with Douglas Jehl, "After War: Militants," *New York Times*, 22 June 2003.

Iraq.[77] U.S. military commanders, moreover, at least as of December had detected no indications of a large number of foreign volunteers converging on Iraq.[78] "It is not correct to say that there are floods of foreign fighters coming in, or thousands," General Abizaid has stated. Indeed, foreign nationals comprise only about 300 of the 5,000 insurgents being held prisoner in Iraq.[79] Bush administration officials, on the other hand, have reportedly estimated the number of foreign jihadists in Iraq at between 1,000 and 3,000—which is also what the Pentagon claims.[80] A similarly high figure was also cited by intelligence officers attached to the Polish-led International Division of coalition forces assigned to the southeast sector of Iraq. They told Cordesman that the main insurgent threat is not from FREs but from foreign jihadists—including at least 500 Ansar al Islam and other non-Iraqis "mixed" in with FREs. Indeed, according to the Division's intelligence officer, a Spaniard, there were some 2,000 foreign volunteers in Iraq, which, as Cordesman notes, "is a notably more precise and higher figure than US intelligence provided."[81] But both American civilian and military officials in Iraq believe that there is nowhere near that number. "A very, very small percentage of foreign fighters," Major General Odierno maintains, are responsible for the attacks on American forces.[82]

Whatever the number of FREs compared with foreign jihadists,[83] it appears clear the violence is worsening. Indeed, to a great extent numbers in this respect are immaterial. For 20 years, a hardcore of just 20 to 30 members of the Red Army Faction (Baader Meinhof Gang) effectively terrorized West Germany—a country far more stable and with more sophisticated, advanced, and reliable police, security, and intelligence services than Iraq is likely to possess at least for some time. Similarly, some 50 to 75 Red Brigadists imposed a reign of terror on Italy; its worst period (the late 1970s) is still referred to as the "years of lead." And for more than 30 years, a dedicated cadre of approximately 200 to 400 IRA gunmen and

---

[77] Ned Parker, "Suicide Bombings in Iraq Blamed on Group of Foreign Fighters," *Agence France Presse*, 30 October 2003. A former senior CIA officer in August reported that U.S. and allied intelligence estimated that 500 to 600 foreign fighters had come to Iraq. See Alissa J. Rubin, "Iraq Seen as Terror Target: Anti-Western extremists have been infiltrating and may be looking to attack symbols of America and its allies, officials say," *Los Angeles Times*, 10 August 2003. See also Michael R. Gordon, "Terror Group Seen as Back Inside Iraq," New York Times, 9 August 2003.

[78] General Abizaid was reported to have said in November that FREs and not foreign terrorists "pose the greatest danger to American troops and to stability in Iraq." Schmitt and Sanger, "Guerrillas Posing More Danger, Says U.S."

[79] Quoted in Desmond Butler and Don Van Natta, Jr., "Recruiters: Trail of Anti-U.S. Fighters Said to Cross Europe to Iraq," *New York Times*, 6 December 2003. This figure dovetails with that provided by Ambassador Bremer in September, when he reported that 248 foreign fighters had been apprehended in Iraq, of whom 19 were members of al Qaeda and 123 were from Syria alone. See Douglas Jehl, "Bremer Says 19 Qaeda Fighters Are in U.S. Custody in Iraq," *New York Times*, 26 September 2003. The number of al Qaeda detainees in November had increased by only one to 20, according to Lieutenant General Sanchez. See Brian Knowlton, "Iraqi Security Forces Outnumber American Troops, U.S. Says," *International Herald Tribune* (Paris), 11 November 2003. The 300 figure was also cited by American officials in December. See Desmond Butler and Don Van Natta, Jr., "Recruiters: Trail of Anti-U.S. Fighters Said to Cross Europe to Iraq," *New York Times*, 6 December 2003.

[80] Bonner and Brinkley, "Latest Attacks Underscore Differing Intelligence Estimates of Strength of Foreign Guerrillas." In September, "American military, intelligence and law enforcement figures" had put the number of foreign fighters at "as many as 1,000." See Eric Schmitt, "Iraq Bombings Pose a Mystery U.S. Must Solve," *New York Times*, 7 September 2003.

[81] Cordesman, *The Current Military Situation in Iraq*, p. 7.

[82] Quoted in Bonner and Brinkley, "Latest Attacks Underscore Differing Intelligence Estimates of Strength of Foreign Guerrillas."

[83] And, in this context, it is argued that domestic American politics influence the depiction of the insurgency problem in Iraq variously as the product of FREs or foreign jihadists. For example, an account published in *Time* magazine explained that "The Bush Administration, for its part, wants to portray the insurgency as mainly homegrown. That allows Washington to claim, as it repeatedly does, that when the die-hards run out of men and munitions, the insurgency will dissipate. It also allows Bush to avoid the charge that the war actually increased danger to the U.S. by stirring up a hornet's nest of terrorism." Bennett and Ware, "Life Behind Enemy Lines." See also Steven R. Weisman, "U.S. Presidential Politics and Self-Rule for Iraqis," *New York Times*, 18 February 2004.

bombers[84] frustrated the maintenance of law and order in Northern Ireland, requiring the prolonged deployment of tens of thousands of British troops in that embattled province.[85]

Where numbers *do* matter is in respect to number of attacks, number of casualties, and the less easily calculated but more profound impact that this violence has on the Iraqi people's sense of security and confidence. In these respects, both the numbers and the impact are disquieting. By early November, U.S. military commanders in Iraq were themselves painting a grim picture. According to Lieutenant General Sanchez, the average number of attacks on American forces had grown from five per day in June to "the teens" in September to 30–35 in October[86] and to 40 by the end of November.[87] The capture of Saddam Hussein in mid-December, however, brought newfound optimism that a decisive corner had been turned in the violence which, it was hoped, would now decline—even though Hussein maintained, and it is believed, that he played no active role in directing the insurgency.[88] Nonetheless, the symbolic value of his apprehension was thought to have greater significance.[89] Indeed, a month later, U.S. military officials in Iraq were already pointing to declines both in insurgent attacks and American military casualties. The average number of daily attacks, they said, had fallen from 23 during the four weeks preceding Hussein's capture to 18 in the four weeks since he was found. Still better news was that U.S. combat injuries had declined as well (though only slightly)—from 233 to 224 over the same time period—prompting Brigadier General Mark Hertling, assistant commander of the 1st Armored Division, to declare, "We are winning this fight." At the same time, however, it is more significant to note that more American troops—31—were killed by insurgents between 14 December 2003 and 10 January 2004 than between 16 November and 13 December, when 22 lost their lives in insurgent attacks.[90] Viewed from this perspective, the news is far less salutary: Despite the fact that the number of attacks declined by 22 percent over this time period, the number of fatalities actually increased by 41 percent. Accordingly, one can make the argument that the insurgents' killing efficiency and the effectiveness of their attacks in fact improved and that Hussein's capture did not have the impact many assumed or hoped that it would.[91]

---

[84] U.S. Department of Defense, *Terrorist Group Profiles* (Washington, D.C.: U.S. Government Printing Office, 1988), pp. 56, 61, 64.

[85] Significantly, to maintain stability and order in Northern Ireland, the ratio of British security forces maintained in Northern Ireland (military plus police from the Royal Ulster Constabulary) was at a ratio of 20 security force members per 1,000 inhabitants. In Iraq, the ratio of coalition military forces to population is a considerably lower 6.1 per 1,000 inhabitants. See James T. Quinlivan, "Burden of Victory: The Painful Arithmetic of Stability Operations," *RAND Review*, Vol. 27, No. 2 (Summer 2003), pp. 28–29. See also, idem, "Force Requirements in Stability Operations," *Parameters* (Winter 1995), pp. 59–69, available online at http://carlisle-www.army.mil/usawc/parameters/1995/quinliv.htm. In a November op-ed, Edward Luttwak further underscored the inadequacy of military forces deployed to Iraq noting that "The support echelon is so large that out of the 133,000 American men and women in Iraq, no more than 56,000 are combat-trained troops available for security duties. . . . For comparison, there are 39,000 police officers in New York City and they at least know the languages of most of the inhabitants, few of whom are likely to be armed Ba'athist fanatics." Idem, "So Few Soldiers, So Much to Do," *New York Times*, 4 November 2003.

[86] John F. Burns, "General Vows to Intensify U.S. Response to Attackers," *New York Times*, 12 November 2003.

[87] Thom Shanker, "Rumsfeld, on the Ground in Iraq, Gets a Report on Progress Against the Insurgency," *New York Times*, 7 December 2003.

[88] Thom Shanker and James Risen, "Hussein Tells Interrogators He Didn't Direct Insurgency," *New York Times*, 15 December 2003.

[89] See Michael R. Gordon, "For U.S. Foes, a Major Blow: Fighters Now Lack a Symbol," *New York Times*, 14 December 2003.

[90] Figures and Brigadier General Hertling quoted in Jim Michaels, "Attacks down 22% since Saddam's capture," *USA Today* (Washington, D.C.), 12 January 2004.

[91] Email correspondence with Christopher Dickey, *Newsweek*'s Paris bureau chief, 2 February 2004.

The same point essentially was made in a recent article in *The Economist*, which reported that during January insurgents had killed 51 coalition troops—the second highest monthly death toll since President Bush declared the war in Iraq over last May. This raised the average daily number of military fatalities to 1.65 from 1.1 in September. Again, an asymmetry was apparent in presumed coalition force successes and improvements compared with growing insurgent lethality. For example, American officials cited an improved detection of roadside bombs and other improvised explosive devices (IEDs) from the 40 percent spotted and safely defused during December to the 60 percent in January; yet the insurgents were nonetheless able to kill more troops that month than in any other of the previous nine months but one. Though not stated as such, this disparity was nonetheless noted, "in a military bulletin on February 6th, some 73 attempted strikes in one day against coalition targets (including Iraqi helpers) were acknowledged: the insurgents, it observed, had 'become more sophisticated and may be co-ordinating their anti-coalition efforts, posing an even more significant threat'."[92] More ominous, perhaps, was the rise in suicide terrorist attacks in Iraq during this period. According to Professor Scott Atran, "Suicide terror now plagues Iraq for the first time since the 13th-century Assassins. From Jan. 14 to Feb. 11, Iraq suffered nine suicide bombings, killing more (257) than in any country for any monthly period since 9/11."[93] News of the mass casualties inflicted on Shi'a worshippers in Baghdad and Karbala on 2 March, their holy day of Ashura, in which at least 117 persons were killed (143 according to the Iraqi Governing Council) and more than 400 injured by suicide bombers,[94] will likely only have sustained that pattern of tragedy.

It is a truism of counterinsurgency that a population will give its allegiance to the side that will best protect it. Charles Simpson made exactly this point with reference to Vietnam in his history of the U.S. Army Special Forces. "In the dirty and dangerous business of revolutionary war," he explained,

> the motivation that produces the only real long-lasting effect is not likely to be an ideology, but the elemental consideration of survival. Peasants will support [the guerrillas] . . . if they are convinced that failure to do so will result in death or brutal punishment. They will support the government if and when they are convinced that it *offers them a better life*, and it can and will protect them against the [guerrillas] . . . forever.[95]

Accordingly, the highest imperative of the insurgent is to deprive the population of that sense of security. Through violence and bloodshed, the insurgent seeks to foment a climate of fear by demonstrating the authorities' inability to maintain order and thus highlight its weakness. Spectacular acts of violence, such as the suicide bombings that have rocked Iraq since August, are meant to demoralize the population and undermine trust and confidence in the authorities' ability to protect and defend them. Here, the fundamental asymmetry of the insurgency/counterinsurgency dynamic comes into play: The guerrillas do not have to defeat their opponents militarily; they just have to avoid losing.[96] And, in this respect, the more

---

[92] Figures and quote in "Iraq: The body count—Still going up," *The Economist* (London), 14 February 2004, p. 42.

[93] Scott Atran, "Iraq and Al Qaeda: No Smoking Gun," Letter to the Editor, *New York Times*, 15 February 2004.

[94] Rajiv Chanrasekaran, "Iraq's Shiites Renew Call for Militias," *Washington Post*, 4 March 2004.

[95] Charles Simpson, *Inside the Green Berets: The First Thirty Years* (Novato, Calif.: Presidio Press, 1982), p. 62.

[96] In Iraq, interestingly, success is in the process of being defined by U.S. military commanders in a similar vein. "If we're being held to a standard that the only way to win is have no more bombs go off, we won't live up to that," Brigadier General Hertling conceded. "Our standard is to reduce them every day. This is the hardest thing I've ever done." Quoted in Eric Schmitt, "For G.I.'s, Pride in War Efforts but Doubts About Iraq's Future," *New York Times*, 4 January 2004.

conspicuous the security forces become and the more pervasive its operations, the stronger the insurgency appears to be. Hence, the insurgent banks on the hope that the disruption caused to daily life and commerce by security force operations countermeasures will further alienate the population from the authorities and create an impression of the security forces as oppressors rather than protectors. This is what Major Nagl found following the car bombing of an Iraqi police station last December that killed 24 policemen, 2 women, and 1 child. "The crowd that gathered after the blast," he recalled, "didn't seem angry at the insurgents responsible for the carnage. Instead, many of them blamed the G.I.'s."[97]

In a nutshell, this is what the current struggle in Iraq is all about.[98] This is clearly recognized by U.S. military commanders. "If you don't have security," Brigadier General Hertling observes, "you can't bring back the economic base, and the enemy is still trying to prevent that."[99] Yet this is a battle that the U.S. and coalition forces are not winning—as the quote at the beginning of this section and the mass demonstrations held in Baghdad the day after the Ashura bombings attest. "They promised to liberate us from occupation," an Iraqi insurgent explained to a United Press International reporter in December. The Americans "promised us rights and liberty," he continued, "and my colleagues and I waited to make our decision on whether to fight until we saw how they would act. They should have come and just given us food and some security. . . . It was then that I realized that they had come as occupiers and not as liberators and my colleagues and I then voted to fight."[100]

Conclusion: Counterinsurgency's Future?

"We know we're killing a lot, capturing a lot, collecting arms. We just don't know yet whether that's the same as winning." —Secretary of Defense Donald Rumsfeld[101]

General Abizaid has described the current conflict in Iraq as a "classical guerrilla-type campaign."[102] The reality is that it is not—which doubtless explains why the insurgency is proving so difficult to defeat and the insurgents themselves so resilient. Unlike a "classical guerrilla-type campaign," the Iraq insurgency has no center of gravity. There appears to be no clear leader (or leadership);[103] no attempt to seize and actually hold territory;[104] and no single, defined, or unifying ideology.[105] Most important, there is no identifiable organization.

---

[97] Maass, "Professor Nagl's War."

[98] See, for example, the comments of Raad Khairy al-Barhawi, a Mosul city councilman who says that he wants the "Americans to succeed," but also complains of death threats and therefore wishes that the Americans will leave. Quoted in Filkins, "Attacks on G.I.'s in Mosul Rise as Good Will Fades." As one U.S. Army officer knowledgeable about counterinsurgency also notes, "There's a 'Catch-22' with military-NGO [nongovernmental organization] interface" that affects the security equation. "NGOs," he explained, "need a secure environment to do their job . . . without it they can't do their work. If NGOs can't do their work, then the US military has to tackle more civic action projects to win hearts and minds. Less troops for security makes it harder to get NGOs in the field." Email communication with the author, May 2004.

[99] Quoted in Schmitt, "For G.I.'s, Pride in War Efforts but Doubts About Iraq's Future."

[100] P. Mitchell Prothero, "Iraqi guerillas: 'Why we fight'," *United Press International*, 4 December 2003.

[101] Quoted in Vernon Loeb, "Rumsfeld Seeks Better Intelligence on Iraqi Insurgents."

[102] Quoted in Knowlton, "Top U.S. General in Iraq Sees 'Classical Guerrilla-Type' War."

[103] The infamous Abu Musab Zarqawi clearly has pretensions to such a role, as evidenced by the letter he wrote to bin Laden that was seized by U.S. authorities (see "Text from Abu Mus'ab al-Zarqawi Letter," accessed at http://www.cpa-iraq.org/transcripts/20040212_zarqawi_full.html), but has yet to merit or achieve such a distinction.

[104] Email communication with a senior CPA official, Baghdad, Iraq, February 2004.

[105] Knights and White, "Iraqi resistance proves resilient," p. 20.

Indeed, none of the four stages of an insurgency defined in the CIA's renowned *Guide to the Analysis of Insurgency* seem to be relevant to the situation in Iraq. These are

- *Preinsurgency*—Leadership emerges in response to domestic grievances or outside influences;
- *Organizational*—Infrastructure built, guerrillas recruited and trained, supplies acquired, and domestic and international support sought;
- *Guerrilla warfare*—Hit-and-run tactics used to attack government. Extensive insurgent political activity—both domestic and international—may also occur simultaneously during this stage;
- *Mobile conventional warfare*—Larger units used in conventional warfare mode. Many insurgencies never reach this stage.[106]

Rather, what we find in Iraq is the closest manifestation yet of *netwar*, the concept of warfare involving flatter, more linear networks rather than the pyramidal hierarchies and command and control systems (no matter how primitive) that have governed traditional insurgent organizations.

Netwar, as defined by the term's originators, John Arquilla and David Ronfeldt, involves "small groups who communicate, coordinate, and conduct their campaigns in an internetted manner, without a precise central command."[107] This description comes closest to explaining the insurgent phenomena that has unfolded in Iraq since August 2003.[108] It is a situation where secular Ba'athists and other FREs increasingly cooperate with religious extremist foreign jihadists along with domestic (Iraqi) jihadists. In this loose, ambiguous, and constantly shifting environment, constellations of cells or collections of individuals gravitate toward one another to carry out armed attacks, exchange intelligence, trade weapons, or engage in joint training and then disperse at times never to operate together again. "Here the Ba'athist/Islamic divide does not exist in a practical sense," according to a senior CPA official with direct knowledge and experience of this matter. "I wouldn't have thought it possible as they were so diametrically opposed to each other during the [Saddam Hussein] regime—but it is happening."[109]

Accordingly, watching and studying the monumental film *The Battle of Algiers*, as Pentagon officials were reported to have done last September,[110] is largely irrelevant to an enemy organized in this loose, amorphous manner. In one of the film's most compelling scenes, its main protagonist, the French paratroop commander, Lieutenant Colonel Mathieu, depicts on a blackboard the cellular structure of the FLN terrorist organization against whom they were fighting. This was described by Alistair Horne, in his seminal work on the conflict, *A Savage War of Peace*, as a "complex *organigramme* [that] began to take shape on a large

---

[106] Central Intelligence Agency, *Guide to the Analysis of Insurgency* (Washington, D.C.: U.S. Government Printing Office, no date), p. 3.

[107] John Arquilla, David Ronfeldt, and Michele Zanini, "Networks, Netwar, and Information-Age Terrorism," in Ian O. Lesser et al., *Countering the New Terrorism* (Santa Monica, Calif.: The RAND Corporation, MR-989-AF, 1999), p. 47.

[108] It should be noted that the netwar concept as explicated by Arquilla and Ronfeldt envisioned technologically adept and information technology–savvy adversaries, exploiting IT for offensive and defensive operations. This aspect of network is certainly not apparent in Iraq.

[109] Email communication with a senior CPA official, Baghdad, Iraq, February 2004.

[110] See, for example, Michael T. Kaufman, "What Does the Pentagon See in 'Battle of Algiers'?" *New York Times*, 7 September 2003; Philip Gourevitch, "Comment: Winning And Losing," *The New Yorker*, 22 and 29 December 2003; and, Stuart Klawans, "Lessons of the Pentagon's Favorite Training Film," *New York Times Sunday Arts and Leisure Section*, 4 January 2004.

blackboard, a kind of skeleton pyramid in which, as each fresh piece of information came from the interrogation centres, another name (and not always necessarily the right name) would be entered."[111] The problem in Iraq is that there appears to be no such static wiring diagram or organizational structure to identify, unravel, and systematically dismantle. If that is in fact the case, then our entire strategy and approach may be irrelevant to the real problem at hand. "Iraq reminds us," one U.S. Army Special Forces officer notes, "that the US government must adapt to a formidable opponent that is widely dispersed, decentralized and whose many destructive parts are autonomous, mobile, and highly adaptive."[112]

It is therefore possible that the insurgency in Iraq may indeed represent a new form of warfare for a new, networked century. It is too soon to determine whether this development, involving loose networks of combatants who come together for a discrete purpose only to quickly disperse upon its achievement, will prove to be a lasting or completely ephemeral characteristic of postmodern insurgency. However, if it gains traction and is indeed revealed to be a harbinger of the future, the implications for how military forces train, equip, and organize to meet this challenge and avoid preparing to fight yesterday's (mostly conventional) wars will be of paramount importance.

---

[111] Alistair Horne, *A Savage War of Peace: Algeria 1954–1962* (Harmondsworth: Penguin, 1977), p. 194.

[112] Email communication with U.S. Army Special Forces officer, May 2004.

Made in the USA
Columbia, SC
18 February 2022

56463005R00015